JAZZ PLAY-ALONG®

Book and CD for B♭, E♭, C and Bass Clef Instruments

volume 106

Arranged and Produced by Mark Taylor

9 JAZZ BALLADS

TITLE	PAGE NUMBERS			
	C Treble Instruments	B♭ Instruments	E♭ Instruments	C Bass Instruments
Don't Blame Me	4	18	32	46
Dreamsville	5	19	33	47
Goodbye	6	20	34	48
I Guess I'll Hang My Tears Out to Dry	8	22	36	50
I'll Be Around	10	24	38	52
I'm Old Fashioned	12	26	40	54
Moonglow	11	25	39	53
My Ship	14	28	42	56
Spring Can Really Hang You Up the Most	16	30	44	58

TITLE	CD Track Number Split Track / Melody	CD Track Number Full Stereo Track
Don't Blame Me	1	2
Dreamsville	3	4
Goodbye	5	6
I Guess I'll Hang My Tears Out to Dry	7	8
I'll Be Around	9	10
I'm Old Fashioned	11	12
Moonglow	13	14
My Ship	15	16
Spring Can Really Hang You Up the Most	17	18
B♭ Tuning Notes		19

ISBN 978-1-4234-5619-3

HAL•LEONARD®
CORPORATION

7777 W. BLUEMOUND RD. P.O. BOX 13819 MILWAUKEE, WI 53213

For all works contained herein:
Unauthorized copying, arranging, adapting, recording, Internet posting, public performance,
or other distriibution of the printed or recorded music in this publication is an infringement of copyright.
Infringers are liable under the law.

Visit Hal Leonard Online at
www.halleonard.com

SLO' JAZZ

Volume 106

Arranged and Produced by
Mark Taylor

Featured Players:

Graham Breedlove–Trumpet
John Desalme–Tenor Saxophone
Tony Nalker–Piano
Jim Roberts–Bass
Leonard Cuddy–Drums

**Recorded at Bias Studios, Springfield, Virginia
Bob Dawson, Engineer**

HOW TO USE THE CD:

Each song has <u>two</u> tracks:

1) Split Track/Melody

Woodwind, Brass, Keyboard, and **Mallet Players** can use this track as a learning tool for melody style and inflection.

Bass Players can learn and perform with this track – remove the recorded bass track by turning down the volume on the LEFT channel.

Keyboard and **Guitar Players** can learn and perform with this track – remove the recorded piano part by turning down the volume on the RIGHT channel.

2) Full Stereo Track

Soloists or **Groups** can learn and perform with this accompaniment track with the RHYTHM SECTION only.

Copyright © 1932 Aldi Music and EMI Robbins Music Corporation
Copyright Renewed
This arrangement Copyright © 2008 Aldi Music and EMI Robbins Music Corporation
Print Rights for Aldi Music in the U.S. Controlled and Administered by Happy Aspen Music LLC c/o Shapiro, Bernstein & Co., Inc.
International Copyright Secured   All Rights Reserved
Used by Permission

DREAMSVILLE

LYRICS BY JAY LIVINGSTON AND RAY EVANS
MUSIC BY HENRY MANCINI

Copyright © 1959 NORTHRIDGE MUSIC CO., ST. ANGELO MUSIC and JAY LIVINGSTON MUSIC
Copyright Renewed
This arrangement Copyright © 2008 NORTHRIDGE MUSIC CO., ST. ANGELO MUSIC and JAY LIVINGSTON MUSIC
All Rights for NORTHRIDGE MUSIC CO. and ST. ANGELO MUSIC Controlled and Administered by UNIVERSAL MUSIC CORP.
All Rights Reserved   Used by Permission

GOODBYE

WORDS AND MUSIC BY
GORDON JENKINS

CD
5 : SPLIT TRACK/MELODY
6 : FULL STEREO TRACK

C VERSION

SLOW BOSSA

Copyright © 1935 LaSALLE MUSIC PUBLISHERS, INC.
Copyright Renewed, Assigned to UNIVERSAL MUSIC CORP.
This arrangement Copyright © 2008 UNIVERSAL MUSIC CORP.
All Rights Reserved   Used by Permission

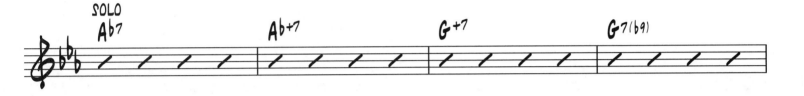

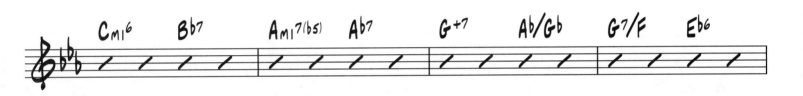

CD
7 : SPLIT TRACK/MELODY
8 : FULL STEREO TRACK

I GUESS I'LL HANG MY TEARS OUT TO DRY

FROM GLAD TO SEE YOU

C VERSION

WORDS BY SAMMY CAHN
MUSIC BY JULE STYNE

Copyright © 1944 Cahn Music Company and Chappell & Co.
Copyright Renewed
This arrangement Copyright © 2008 Cahn Music Company and Chappell & Co.
International Copyright Secured   All Rights Reserved

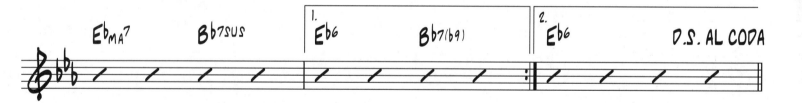

I'LL BE AROUND

CD
◆9 : SPLIT TRACK/MELODY
◆10 : FULL STEREO TRACK

WORDS AND MUSIC BY
ALEC WILDER

C VERSION

TRO - © Copyright 1942 (Renewed) Ludlow Music, Inc., New York, NY
This arrangement TRO - © Copyright 2008 Ludlow Music, Inc., New York, NY
International Copyright Secured
All Rights Reserved Including Public Performance For Profit
Used by Permission

MOONGLOW

WORDS AND MUSIC BY WILL HUDSON,
EDDIE DE LANGE AND IRVING MILLS

Copyright © 1934 Mills Music, Inc., New York
Copyright Renewed, Assigned to Mills Music, Inc. and Scarsdale Music Corporation, New York for the United States
This arrangement Copyright © 2008 Mills Music, Inc. and Scarsdale Music Corporation, New York for the United States
All Rights outside the United States Controlled by Mills Music, Inc.
International Copyright Secured   All Rights Reserved
Used by Permission

CD
11 : SPLIT TRACK/MELODY
12 : FULL STEREO TRACK

I'M OLD FASHIONED
FROM YOU WERE NEVER LOVELIER

WORDS BY JOHNNY MERCER
MUSIC BY JEROME KERN

C VERSION

Copyright © 1942 UNIVERSAL - POLYGRAM INTERNATIONAL PUBLISHING, INC.
Copyright Renewed
This arrangement Copyright © 2008 UNIVERSAL - POLYGRAM INTERNATIONAL PUBLISHING, INC.
All Rights Reserved   Used by Permission

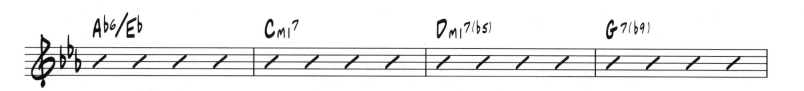

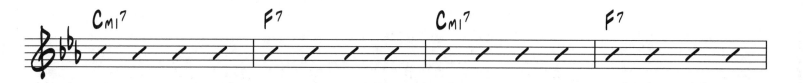

MY SHIP
FROM THE MUSICAL PRODUCTION LADY IN THE DARK

WORDS BY IRA GERSHWIN
MUSIC BY KURT WEILL

C VERSION

TRO - © Copyright 1941 (Renewed) Hampshire House Publishing Corp., New York and Chappell & Co., Los Angeles, CA
This arrangement TRO - © Copyright 2008 Hampshire House Publishing Corp., New York and Chappell & Co., Los Angeles, CA
International Copyright Secured
All Rights Reserved Including Public Performance For Profit
Used by Permission

TO CODA ⊕

SOLO

F6   D7(b9)   G7   C7SUS   F6   D7(b9) /C   Bmi7(b5)   Bb7

Ami7   D+7   Gmi7   Fmi7   Emi7   A7   1. Dmi7   G7

Gmi7   C7   Db7   C7(b9)   2. Dmi7   G7   C7SUS   F6   D.S. AL CODA

⊕ CODA

Dmi7   C7   FMA7   Gmi7   C7   FMA7   B7

Bb7   Eb7 /Bb   Ami7   Ab7   Gmi7   C7(b9)   GbMA7   F6

SPRING CAN REALLY HANG YOU UP THE MOST

CD

◆17: SPLIT TRACK/MELODY
◆18: FULL STEREO TRACK

LYRIC BY FRAN LANDESMAN
MUSIC BY TOMMY WOLF

C VERSION

Copyright © 1955 by Wolf Mills, Inc., c/o Fricout Music Company, 134 Bluegrass Circle, Hendersonville, TN 37075
Copyright Renewed
Copyright © 1987 Assigned to WOLFLAND, Admin. by Fricout Music Company, 134 Bluegrass Circle, Hendersonville, TN 37075
This arrangement Copyright © 2008 WOLFLAND, Admin. by Fricout Music Company, 134 Bluegrass Circle, Hendersonville, TN 37075
International Copyright Secured   All Rights Reserved

DON'T BLAME ME

Copyright © 1932 Aldi Music and EMI Robbins Music Corporation
Copyright Renewed
This arrangement Copyright © 2008 Aldi Music and EMI Robbins Music Corporation
Print Rights for Aldi Music in the U.S. Controlled and Administered by Happy Aspen Music LLC c/o Shapiro, Bernstein & Co., Inc.
International Copyright Secured   All Rights Reserved
Used by Permission

DREAMSVILLE

CD
❸ : SPLIT TRACK/MELODY
❹ : FULL STEREO TRACK

LYRICS BY JAY LIVINGSTON AND RAY EVANS
MUSIC BY HENRY MANCINI

Bb VERSION

Copyright © 1959 NORTHRIDGE MUSIC CO., ST. ANGELO MUSIC and JAY LIVINGSTON MUSIC
Copyright Renewed
This arrangement Copyright © 2008 NORTHRIDGE MUSIC CO., ST. ANGELO MUSIC and JAY LIVINGSTON MUSIC
All Rights for NORTHRIDGE MUSIC CO. and ST. ANGELO MUSIC Controlled and Administered by UNIVERSAL MUSIC CORP.
All Rights Reserved   Used by Permission

GOODBYE

Copyright © 1935 LaSALLE MUSIC PUBLISHERS, INC.
Copyright Renewed, Assigned to UNIVERSAL MUSIC CORP.
This arrangement Copyright © 2008 UNIVERSAL MUSIC CORP.
All Rights Reserved   Used by Permission

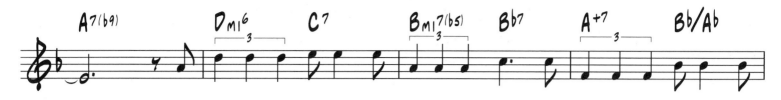

CD
7 : SPLIT TRACK/MELODY
8 : FULL STEREO TRACK

I GUESS I'LL HANG MY TEARS OUT TO DRY

FROM GLAD TO SEE YOU

Bb VERSION

WORDS BY SAMMY CAHN
MUSIC BY JULE STYNE

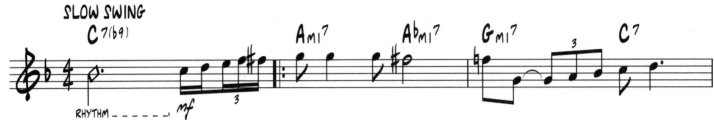

Copyright © 1944 Cahn Music Company and Chappell & Co.
Copyright Renewed
This arrangement Copyright © 2008 Cahn Music Company and Chappell & Co.
International Copyright Secured   All Rights Reserved

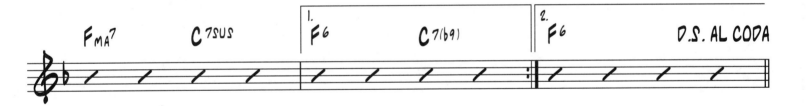

I'LL BE AROUND

WORDS AND MUSIC BY
ALEC WILDER

TRO - © Copyright 1942 (Renewed) Ludlow Music, Inc., New York, NY
This arrangement TRO - © Copyright 2008 Ludlow Music, Inc., New York, NY
International Copyright Secured
All Rights Reserved Including Public Performance For Profit
Used by Permission

MOONGLOW

WORDS AND MUSIC BY WILL HUDSON,
EDDIE DE LANGE AND IRVING MILLS

Copyright © 1934 Mills Music, Inc., New York
Copyright Renewed, Assigned to Mills Music, Inc. and Scarsdale Music Corporation, New York for the United States
This arrangement Copyright © 2008 Mills Music, Inc. and Scarsdale Music Corporation, New York for the United States
All Rights outside the United States Controlled by Mills Music, Inc.
International Copyright Secured   All Rights Reserved
Used by Permission

I'M OLD FASHIONED

FROM YOU WERE NEVER LOVELIER

WORDS BY JOHNNY MERCER
MUSIC BY JEROME KERN

CD
11 : SPLIT TRACK/MELODY
12 : FULL STEREO TRACK

Bb VERSION

Copyright © 1942 UNIVERSAL - POLYGRAM INTERNATIONAL PUBLISHING, INC.
Copyright Renewed
This arrangement Copyright © 2008 UNIVERSAL - POLYGRAM INTERNATIONAL PUBLISHING, INC.
All Rights Reserved   Used by Permission

SOLO

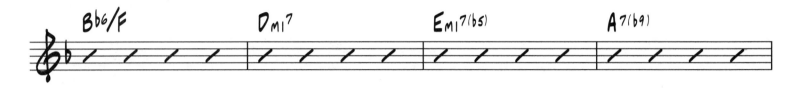

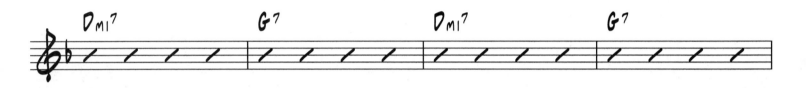

D.S. AL CODA

MY SHIP
FROM THE MUSICAL PRODUCTION LADY IN THE DARK

WORDS BY IRA GERSHWIN
MUSIC BY KURT WEILL

TRO - © Copyright 1941 (Renewed) Hampshire House Publishing Corp., New York and Chappell & Co., Los Angeles, CA
This arrangement TRO - © Copyright 2008 Hampshire House Publishing Corp., New York and Chappell & Co., Los Angeles, CA
International Copyright Secured
All Rights Reserved Including Public Performance For Profit
Used by Permission

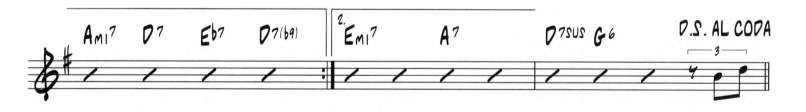

CD
17 : SPLIT TRACK/MELODY
18 : FULL STEREO TRACK

SPRING CAN REALLY HANG YOU UP THE MOST

LYRIC BY FRAN LANDESMAN
MUSIC BY TOMMY WOLF

Bb VERSION

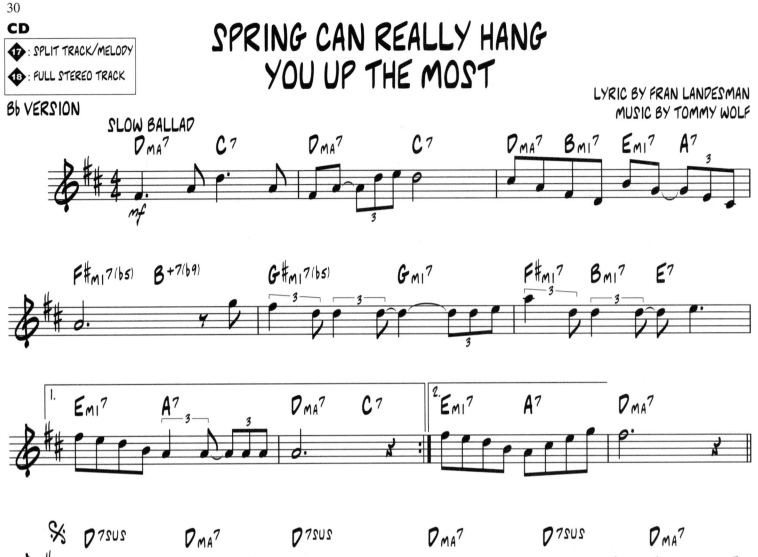

Copyright © 1955 by Wolf Mills, Inc., c/o Fricout Music Company, 134 Bluegrass Circle, Hendersonville, TN 37075
Copyright Renewed
Copyright © 1987 Assigned to WOLFLAND, Admin. by Fricout Music Company, 134 Bluegrass Circle, Hendersonville, TN 37075
This arrangement Copyright © 2008 WOLFLAND, Admin. by Fricout Music Company, 134 Bluegrass Circle, Hendersonville, TN 37075
International Copyright Secured   All Rights Reserved

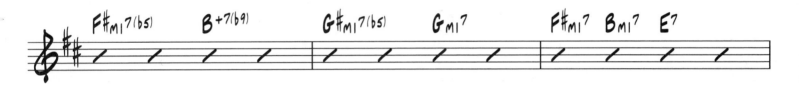

DON'T BLAME ME

CD
1 : SPLIT TRACK/MELODY
2 : FULL STEREO TRACK

WORDS BY DOROTHY FIELDS
MUSIC BY JIMMY McHUGH

Eb VERSION

Copyright © 1932 Aldi Music and EMI Robbins Music Corporation
Copyright Renewed
This arrangement Copyright © 2008 Aldi Music and EMI Robbins Music Corporation
Print Rights for Aldi Music in the U.S. Controlled and Administered by Happy Aspen Music LLC c/o Shapiro, Bernstein & Co., Inc.
International Copyright Secured   All Rights Reserved
Used by Permission

Dreamsville

LYRICS BY JAY LIVINGSTON AND RAY EVANS
MUSIC BY HENRY MANCINI

Copyright © 1959 NORTHRIDGE MUSIC CO., ST. ANGELO MUSIC and JAY LIVINGSTON MUSIC
Copyright Renewed
This arrangement Copyright © 2008 NORTHRIDGE MUSIC CO., ST. ANGELO MUSIC and JAY LIVINGSTON MUSIC
All Rights for NORTHRIDGE MUSIC CO. and ST. ANGELO MUSIC Controlled and Administered by UNIVERSAL MUSIC CORP.
All Rights Reserved   Used by Permission

CD
◆**5** : SPLIT TRACK/MELODY
◆**6** : FULL STEREO TRACK

GOODBYE

WORDS AND MUSIC BY
GORDON JENKINS

Eb VERSION

SLOW BOSSA

Copyright © 1935 LaSALLE MUSIC PUBLISHERS, INC.
Copyright Renewed, Assigned to UNIVERSAL MUSIC CORP.
This arrangement Copyright © 2008 UNIVERSAL MUSIC CORP.
All Rights Reserved   Used by Permission

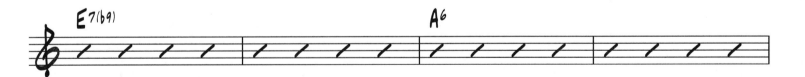

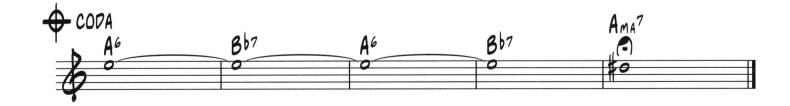

CD
- **7** : SPLIT TRACK/MELODY
- **8** : FULL STEREO TRACK

I GUESS I'LL HANG MY TEARS OUT TO DRY

FROM GLAD TO SEE YOU

WORDS BY SAMMY CAHN
MUSIC BY JULE STYNE

Eb VERSION

Copyright © 1944 Cahn Music Company and Chappell & Co.
Copyright Renewed
This arrangement Copyright © 2008 Cahn Music Company and Chappell & Co.
International Copyright Secured   All Rights Reserved

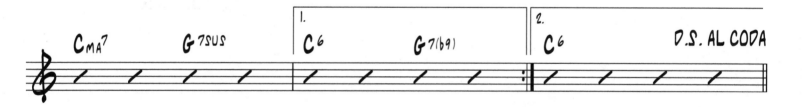

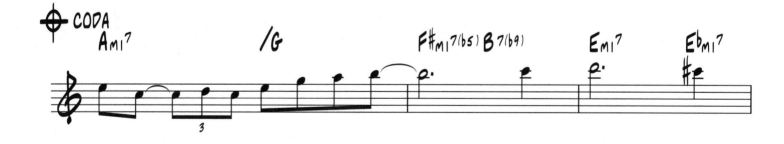

I'LL BE AROUND

WORDS AND MUSIC BY
ALEC WILDER

Eb VERSION

TRO - © Copyright 1942 (Renewed) Ludlow Music, Inc., New York, NY
This arrangement TRO - © Copyright 2008 Ludlow Music, Inc., New York, NY
International Copyright Secured
All Rights Reserved Including Public Performance For Profit
Used by Permission

MOONGLOW

WORDS AND MUSIC BY WILL HUDSON,
EDDIE DE LANGE AND IRVING MILLS

Copyright © 1934 Mills Music, Inc., New York
Copyright Renewed, Assigned to Mills Music, Inc. and Scarsdale Music Corporation, New York for the United States
This arrangement Copyright © 2008 Mills Music, Inc. and Scarsdale Music Corporation, New York for the United States
All Rights outside the United States Controlled by Mills Music, Inc.
International Copyright Secured   All Rights Reserved
Used by Permission

I'M OLD FASHIONED
FROM YOU WERE NEVER LOVELIER

WORDS BY JOHNNY MERCER
MUSIC BY JEROME KERN

Copyright © 1942 UNIVERSAL - POLYGRAM INTERNATIONAL PUBLISHING, INC.
Copyright Renewed
This arrangement Copyright © 2008 UNIVERSAL - POLYGRAM INTERNATIONAL PUBLISHING, INC.
All Rights Reserved   Used by Permission

MY SHIP
FROM THE MUSICAL PRODUCTION LADY IN THE DARK

WORDS BY IRA GERSHWIN
MUSIC BY KURT WEILL

TRO - © Copyright 1941 (Renewed) Hampshire House Publishing Corp., New York and Chappell & Co., Los Angeles, CA
This arrangement TRO - © Copyright 2008 Hampshire House Publishing Corp., New York and Chappell & Co., Los Angeles, CA
International Copyright Secured
All Rights Reserved Including Public Performance For Profit
Used by Permission

CD

🔷17 : SPLIT TRACK/MELODY

🔷18 : FULL STEREO TRACK

SPRING CAN REALLY HANG YOU UP THE MOST

Eb VERSION

LYRIC BY FRAN LANDESMAN
MUSIC BY TOMMY WOLF

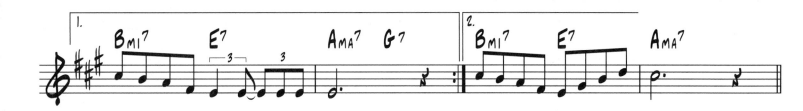

Copyright © 1955 by Wolf Mills, Inc., c/o Fricout Music Company, 134 Bluegrass Circle, Hendersonville, TN 37075
Copyright Renewed
Copyright © 1987 Assigned to WOLFLAND, Admin. by Fricout Music Company, 134 Bluegrass Circle, Hendersonville, TN 37075
This arrangement Copyright © 2008 WOLFLAND, Admin. by Fricout Music Company, 134 Bluegrass Circle, Hendersonville, TN 37075
International Copyright Secured   All Rights Reserved

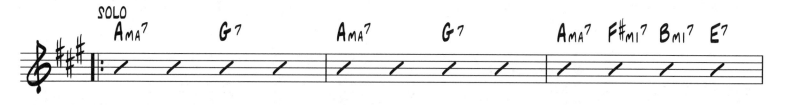

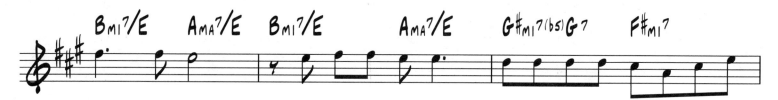

DON'T BLAME ME

WORDS BY DOROTHY FIELDS
MUSIC BY JIMMY McHUGH

Copyright © 1932 Aldi Music and EMI Robbins Music Corporation
Copyright Renewed
This arrangement Copyright © 2008 Aldi Music and EMI Robbins Music Corporation
Print Rights for Aldi Music in the U.S. Controlled and Administered by Happy Aspen Music LLC c/o Shapiro, Bernstein & Co., Inc.
International Copyright Secured   All Rights Reserved
Used by Permission

DREAMSVILLE

LYRICS BY JAY LIVINGSTON AND RAY EVANS
MUSIC BY HENRY MANCINI

Copyright © 1959 NORTHRIDGE MUSIC CO., ST. ANGELO MUSIC and JAY LIVINGSTON MUSIC
Copyright Renewed
This arrangement Copyright © 2008 NORTHRIDGE MUSIC CO., ST. ANGELO MUSIC and JAY LIVINGSTON MUSIC
All Rights for NORTHRIDGE MUSIC CO. and ST. ANGELO MUSIC Controlled and Administered by UNIVERSAL MUSIC CORP.
All Rights Reserved   Used by Permission

GOODBYE

WORDS AND MUSIC BY
GORDON JENKINS

CD
- ◆5 : SPLIT TRACK/MELODY
- ◆6 : FULL STEREO TRACK

𝄢: C VERSION

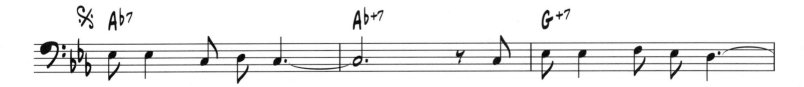

Copyright © 1935 LaSALLE MUSIC PUBLISHERS, INC.
Copyright Renewed, Assigned to UNIVERSAL MUSIC CORP.
This arrangement Copyright © 2008 UNIVERSAL MUSIC CORP.
All Rights Reserved   Used by Permission

CD

7: SPLIT TRACK/MELODY
8: FULL STEREO TRACK

𝄢 : C VERSION

I GUESS I'LL HANG MY TEARS OUT TO DRY

FROM GLAD TO SEE YOU

WORDS BY SAMMY CAHN
MUSIC BY JULE STYNE

SLOW SWING

Copyright © 1944 Cahn Music Company and Chappell & Co.
Copyright Renewed
This arrangement Copyright © 2008 Cahn Music Company and Chappell & Co.
International Copyright Secured   All Rights Reserved

51

I'LL BE AROUND

WORDS AND MUSIC BY
ALEC WILDER

TRO - © Copyright 1942 (Renewed) Ludlow Music, Inc., New York, NY
This arrangement TRO - © Copyright 2008 Ludlow Music, Inc., New York, NY
International Copyright Secured
All Rights Reserved Including Public Performance For Profit
Used by Permission

MOONGLOW

WORDS AND MUSIC BY WILL HUDSON,
EDDIE DE LANGE AND IRVING MILLS

Copyright © 1934 Mills Music, Inc., New York
Copyright Renewed, Assigned to Mills Music, Inc. and Scarsdale Music Corporation, New York for the United States
This arrangement Copyright © 2008 Mills Music, Inc. and Scarsdale Music Corporation, New York for the United States
All Rights outside the United States Controlled by Mills Music, Inc.
International Copyright Secured   All Rights Reserved
Used by Permission

I'M OLD FASHIONED

FROM YOU WERE NEVER LOVELIER

WORDS BY JOHNNY MERCER
MUSIC BY JEROME KERN

Copyright © 1942 UNIVERSAL - POLYGRAM INTERNATIONAL PUBLISHING, INC.
Copyright Renewed
This arrangement Copyright © 2008 UNIVERSAL - POLYGRAM INTERNATIONAL PUBLISHING, INC.
All Rights Reserved   Used by Permission

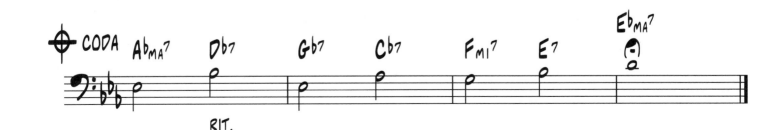

MY SHIP
FROM THE MUSICAL PRODUCTION LADY IN THE DARK

WORDS BY IRA GERSHWIN
MUSIC BY KURT WEILL

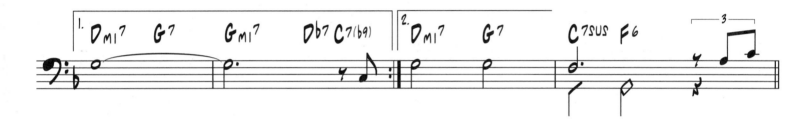

TRO - © Copyright 1941 (Renewed) Hampshire House Publishing Corp., New York and Chappell & Co., Los Angeles, CA
This arrangement TRO - © Copyright 2008 Hampshire House Publishing Corp., New York and Chappell & Co., Los Angeles, CA
International Copyright Secured
All Rights Reserved Including Public Performance For Profit
Used by Permission

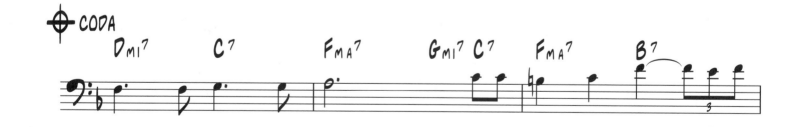

SPRING CAN REALLY HANG YOU UP THE MOST

LYRIC BY FRAN LANDESMAN
MUSIC BY TOMMY WOLF

𝄢 C VERSION

Copyright © 1955 by Wolf Mills, Inc., c/o Fricout Music Company, 134 Bluegrass Circle, Hendersonville, TN 37075
Copyright Renewed
Copyright © 1987 Assigned to WOLFLAND, Admin. by Fricout Music Company, 134 Bluegrass Circle, Hendersonville, TN 37075
This arrangement Copyright © 2008 WOLFLAND, Admin. by Fricout Music Company, 134 Bluegrass Circle, Hendersonville, TN 37075
International Copyright Secured   All Rights Reserved

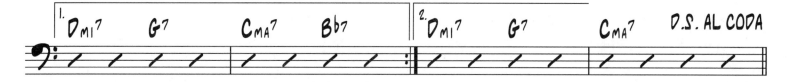

Presenting the Hal Leonard JAZZ PLAY-ALONG SERIES

DUKE ELLINGTON Vol. 1
Caravan • Don't Get Around Much Anymore • In a Sentimental Mood • Perdido • Prelude to a Kiss • Satin Doll • Take the "A" Train • and more.
00841644 ....$16.95

MILES DAVIS Vol. 2
All Blues • Blue in Green • Four • Half Nelson • Milestones • Nardis • Seven Steps to Heaven • So What • Solar • Tune Up.
00841645 ....$16.95

THE BLUES Vol. 3
Billie's Bounce • Birk's Works • C-Jam Blues • Freddie Freeloader • Mr. P.C. • Tenor Madness • Things Ain't What They Used to Be • and more.
00841646 ....$15.95

JAZZ BALLADS Vol. 4
Body and Soul • Here's That Rainy Day • Misty • My Funny Valentine • The Nearness of You • Polka Dots and Moonbeams • and more.
00841691 ....$15.95

BEST OF BEBOP Vol. 5
Anthropology • Donna Lee • Doxy • Epistrophy • Lady Bird • Oleo • Ornithology • Scrapple from the Apple • Woodyn' You • Yardbird Suite.
00841689 ....$15.95

JAZZ CLASSICS WITH EASY CHANGES Vol. 6
Blue Train • Comin' Home Baby • Footprints • Impressions • Killer Joe • St. Thomas • Well You Needn't • and more.
00841690 ....$15.95

ESSENTIAL JAZZ STANDARDS Vol. 7
Autumn Leaves • Lullaby of Birdland • Stella by Starlight • There Will Never Be Another You • When Sunny Gets Blue • and more.
00843000 ....$15.95

ANTONIO CARLOS JOBIM AND THE ART OF THE BOSSA NOVA Vol. 8
The Girl from Ipanema • How Insensitive • Meditation • One Note Samba • Quiet Nights of Quiet Stars • Slightly Out of Tune • and more.
00843001 ....$16.95

DIZZY GILLESPIE Vol. 9
Birk's Works • Con Alma • Groovin' High • Manteca • A Night in Tunisia • Salt Peanuts • Tour De Force • Woodyn' You • and more.
00843002 ....$15.95

DISNEY CLASSICS Vol. 10
Alice in Wonderland • Cruella De Vil • When You Wish upon a Star • You've Got a Friend in Me • Zip-a-Dee-Doo-Dah • and more.
00843003 ....$15.95

RODGERS AND HART FAVORITES Vol. 11
Bewitched • Dancing on the Ceiling • Have You Met Miss Jones? • I Could Write a Book • The Lady Is a Tramp • My Romance • and more.
00843004 ....$15.95

ESSENTIAL JAZZ CLASSICS Vol. 12
Airegin • Ceora • The Frim Fram Sauce • Israel • Milestones • Nefertiti • Red Clay • Satin Doll • Song for My Father • Take Five.
00843005 ....$15.95

JOHN COLTRANE Vol. 13
Blue Train • Countdown • Cousin Mary • Equinox • Giant Steps • Impressions • Lazy Bird • Mr. P.C. • Moment's Notice • Naima.
00843006 ....$16.95

IRVING BERLIN Vol. 14
Blue Skies • How Deep Is the Ocean • I've Got My Love to Keep Me Warm • Steppin' Out with My Baby • What'll I Do? • and more.
00843007 ....$14.95

RODGERS & HAMMERSTEIN Vol. 15
Do I Love You Because You're Beautiful? • It Might as Well Be Spring • My Favorite Things • Younger than Springtime • and more.
00843008 ....$14.95

COLE PORTER Vol. 16
Easy to Love • I Concentrate on You • I've Got You Under My Skin • It's All Right with Me • It's De-Lovely • You'd Be So Nice to Come Home To • and more.
00843009 ....$15.95

COUNT BASIE Vol. 17
All of Me • April in Paris • Blues in Hoss Flat • Li'l Darlin' • Moten Swing • One O'Clock Jump • Shiny Stockings • Until I Met You • and more.
00843010 ....$16.95

HAROLD ARLEN Vol. 18
Ac-cent-tchu-ate the Positive • Come Rain or Come Shine • I've Got the World on a String • Stormy Weather • That Old Black Magic • and more.
00843011 ....$16.95

COOL JAZZ Vol. 19
Bernie's Tune • Boplicity • Budo • Conception • Django • Five Brothers • Line for Lyons • Walkin' Shoes • Waltz for Debby • Whisper Not.
00843012 ....$15.95

CHRISTMAS CAROLS Vol. 20
Away in a Manger • Greensleeves • Hark! the Herald Angels Sing • Joy to the World • O Little Town of Bethlehem • Silent Night • more.
00843080 ....$14.95

RODGERS AND HART CLASSICS Vol. 21
Falling in Love with Love • Isn't it Romantic? • Manhattan • My Funny Valentine • This Can't Be Love • Thou Swell • Where or When • and more.
00843014 ....$14.95

WAYNE SHORTER Vol. 22
Children of the Night • ESP • Footprints • Juju • Mahjong • Nefertiti • Nightdreamer • Speak No Evil • Witch Hunt • Yes and No.
00843015 ....$16.95

LATIN JAZZ Vol. 23
Agua De Beber • Chega De Saudade • Manha De Carnaval • Mas Que Nada • Ran Kan Kan • So Nice • Watch What Happens • and more.
00843016 ....$16.95

EARLY JAZZ STANDARDS Vol. 24
After You've Gone • Avalon • Indian Summer • Indiana • Ja-Da • Limehouse Blues • Paper Doll • Poor Butterfly • Rose Room • St. Louis Blues.
00843017 ....$14.95

CHRISTMAS JAZZ Vol. 25
The Christmas Song (Chestnuts Roasting on an Open Fire) • I'll Be Home for Christmas • Let It Snow! Let It Snow! Let It Snow! • Silver Bells • and more.
00843018 ....$16.95

CHARLIE PARKER Vol. 26
Au Privave • Billie's Bounce • Donna Lee • My Little Suede Shoes • Ornithology • Scrapple from the Apple • Yardbird Suite • and more.
00843019 ....$16.95

GREAT JAZZ STANDARDS Vol. 27
Fly Me to the Moon • How High the Moon • I Can't Get Started with You • Speak Low • Tangerine • Willow Weep for Me • and more.
00843020 ....$14.95

BIG BAND ERA Vol. 28
Air Mail Special • Christopher Columbus • In the Mood • Jersey Bounce • Opus One • Stompin' at the Savoy • Tuxedo Junction • and more.
00843021 ....$14.95

LENNON AND McCARTNEY Vol. 29
And I Love Her • Blackbird • Come Together • Eleanor Rigby • Let It Be • Ticket to Ride • Yesterday • and more.
00843022 ....$16.95

BLUES' BEST Vol. 30
Basin Street Blues • Bloomdido • Happy Go Lucky Local • K.C. Blues • Sonnymoon for Two • Take the Coltrane • Turnaround • Twisted • and more.
00843023 ....$14.95

JAZZ IN THREE Vol. 31
Bluesette • Jitterbug Waltz • Moon River • Tennessee Waltz • West Coast Blues • What the World Needs Now Is Love • Wives and Lovers • and more.
00843024 ....$14.95

BEST OF SWING Vol. 32
Alright, Okay, You Win • Cherokee • I'll Be Seeing You • Jump, Jive an' Wail • On the Sunny Side of the Street • Route 66 • Sentimental Journey • and more.
00843025 ....$14.95

SONNY ROLLINS Vol. 33
Airegin • Alfie's Theme • Biji • The Bridge • Doxy • First Moves • Here's to the People • Oleo • St. Thomas • Sonnymoon for Two.
00843029 ....$15.95

ALL TIME STANDARDS Vol. 34
Autumn in New York • Bye Bye Blackbird • Call Me Irresponsible • Georgia on My Mind • Honeysuckle Rose • Stardust • The Very Thought of You • more.
00843030 ....$14.95

BLUESY JAZZ Vol. 35
Angel Eyes • Bags' Groove • Bessie's Blues • Chitlins Con Carne • Mercy, Mercy, Mercy • Night Train • Sweet Georgia Bright • and more.
00843031 ....$14.95

HORACE SILVER Vol. 36
Doodlin' • The Jody Grind • Nica's Dream • Opus De Funk • Peace • The Preacher • Senor Blues • Sister Sadie • Song for My Father • Strollin'.
00843032 ....$15.95

BILL EVANS Vol. 37
Funkallero • My Bells • One for Helen • The Opener • Orbit • Show-Type Tune • 34 Skidoo • Time Remembered • Turn Out the Stars • Waltz for Debby.
00843033 ....$16.95

YULETIDE JAZZ Vol. 38
Blue Christmas • Christmas Time Is Here • Merry Christmas, Darling • The Most Wonderful Time of the Year • Santa Claus Is Comin' to Town • and more.
00843034 ....$15.95

"ALL THE THINGS YOU ARE" & MORE JEROME KERN SONGS Vol. 39
All the Things You Are • Can't Help Lovin' Dat Man • A Fine Romance • Long Ago (And Far Away) • The Way You Look Tonight • Yesterdays • and more.
00843035 ....$14.95

BOSSA NOVA Vol. 40
Black Orpheus • Call Me • A Man and a Woman • Only Trust Your Heart • The Shadow of Your Smile • Watch What Happens • Wave • and more.
00843036 ....$14.95

CLASSIC DUKE ELLINGTON Vol. 41
Cotton Tail • Do Nothin' Till You Hear from Me • I Got It Bad and That Ain't Good • I'm Beginning to See the Light • Mood Indigo • Solitude • and more.
00843037 ....$15.95

GERRY MULLIGAN FAVORITES Vol. 42
Bark for Barksdale • Dragonfly • Elevation • Idol Gossip • Jeru • The Lonely Night (Night Lights) • Noblesse • Rock Salt a/k/a Rocker • Theme for Jobim • Wallflower.
00843038 ....$15.95

GERRY MULLIGAN CLASSICS Vol. 43
Apple Core • Line for Lyons • Nights at the Turntable • Song for Strayhorn • Walkin' Shoes • and more.
00843039 ....$16.95

OLIVER NELSON Vol. 44
The Drive • Emancipation Blues • Hoe-Down • I Remember Bird • Miss Fine • Stolen Moments • Straight Ahead • Teenie's Blues • Yearnin'.
00843040 ....$16.95

JAZZ AT THE MOVIES Vol. 45
Baby Elephant Walk • God Bless' the Child • The Look of Love • The Rainbow Connection • Swinging on a Star • Thanks for the Memory • and more.
00843041 ....$14.95

BROADWAY JAZZ STANDARDS Vol. 46
Ain't Misbehavin' • I've Grown Accustomed to Her Face • Make Someone Happy • Old Devil Moon • Small World • Till There Was You • and more.
00843042 ....$14.95

CLASSIC JAZZ BALLADS Vol. 47
Blame It on My Youth • It's Easy to Remember • June in January • Love Letters • A Nightingale Sang in Berkeley Square • When I Fall in Love • and more.
00843043 ....$14.95

BEBOP CLASSICS Vol. 48
Be-Bop • Bird Feathers • Blue 'N Boogie • Byrd Like • Cool Blues • Dance of the Indifels • Dexterity • Dizzy Atmosphere • Groovin' High • Tempus Fugit.
00843044 ....$15.95

MILES DAVIS STANDARDS Vol. 49
Darn That Dream • I Loves You, Porgy • If I Were a Bell • On Green Dolphin Street • Some Day My Prince Will Come • Yesterdays • and more.
00843045 ....$16.95

GREAT JAZZ CLASSICS Vol. 50
Along Came Betty • Birdland • The Jive Samba • Little Sunflower • Nuages • Peri's Scope • Phase Dance • Road Song • Think on Me • Windows.
00843046 ....$14.95

UP-TEMPO JAZZ Vol. 51
Cherokee (Indian Love Song) • Chi Chi • 52nd Street Theme • Little Willie Leaps • Move • Pent Up House • Topsy • and more.
00843047 ....$14.95

STEVIE WONDER Vol. 52
I Just Called to Say I Love You • Isn't She Lovely • My Cherie Amour • Part Time Lover • Superstition • You Are the Sunshine of My Life • and more.
00843048 ....$15.95

RHYTHM CHANGES Vol. 53
Celia • Chasing the Bird • Cotton Tail • Crazeology • Fox Hunt • I Got Rhythm • No Moe • Oleo • Red Cross • Steeplechase.
00843049 ....$14.95

"MOONLIGHT IN VERMONT" AND OTHER GREAT STANDARDS Vol. 54
A Child Is Born • Love You Madly • Lover Man (Oh, Where Can You Be?) • Moonlight in Vermont • The Night Has a Thousand Eyes • Small Fry • and more.
00843050 ....$14.95

BENNY GOLSON Vol. 55
Along Came Betty • Blues March • Gypsy Jingle-Jangle • I Remember Clifford • Killer Joe • Step Lightly • Whisper Not • and more.
00843052 ....$15.95

VINCE GUARALDI Vol. 57
Blue Charlie Brown • Christmas Time Is Here • Frieda (With the Naturally Curly Hair) • The Great Pumpkin Waltz • Happiness Theme • Linus and Lucy • Oh, Good Grief • The Pebble Beach Theme • Skating • Surfin' Snoopy.
00843057 ....$15.95

MORE LENNON AND McCARTNEY Vol. 58
Can't Buy Me Love • Michelle • Norwegian Wood (This Bird Has Flown) • Eight Days a Week • Yellow Submarine • In My Life • The Long and Winding Road • All My Loving • Julia • Ob-La-Di, Ob-La-Da.
00843059 ....$14.95

SOUL JAZZ Vol. 59
The Cape Verdean Blues • Cold Duck Time • Dat Dere • Freight Trane • Holy Land • The Jive Samba • Nutville • Unit Seven • Work Song.
00843060 ....$14.95

MONGO SANTAMARIA Vol. 61
Afro Blue • Come Candellia • Federico • Las Guajiras • Linda Guajira • Manila • Sabroso • Watermelon Man.
00843062 ....$15.95

JAZZ-ROCK FUSION Vol. 62
Brown Hornet • Chameleon • Got a Match? • Loose Ends • Revelation • Snakes • Spain • Three Views of a Secret • Watermelon Man.
00843063 ....$14.95

CLASSICAL JAZZ Vol. 63
Eine Kleine Nachtmusik • Emperor Waltz • Habanera • Jesu, Joy of Man's Desiring • Minuet in G • New World Symphony (Theme) • Nocturne in F Minor • Ode to Joy • Pavane • Pavane (For a Dead Princess).
00843064 ....$14.95

TV TUNES Vol. 64
Bandstand Boogie • Theme from Family Guy • Theme from Frasier • Hawaii Five-O Theme • Love and Marriage • Mission: Impossible Theme • The Odd Couple • Theme from the Simpsons • Theme from Spider Man • Theme from Star Trek®.
00843065 ....$14.95

SMOOTH JAZZ Vol. 65
Angela • Cast Your Fate to the Wind • Feels So Good • Give Me the Night • Just the Two of Us • Minute by Minute • Morning Dance • Songbird • Street Life • This Masquerade.
00843066 ....$14.95

A CHARLIE BROWN CHRISTMAS Vol. 66
Christmas Is Coming • The Christmas Song (Chestnuts Roasting on an Open Fire) • Christmas Time Is Here • Linus and Lucy • My Little Drum • O Tannenbaum • Skating • What Child Is This.
00843067 ....$15.95

CHICK COREA Vol. 67
Bud Powell • Captain Marvel • 500 Miles High • Litha • The Loop • Mirror, Mirror • Now He Beats the Drum, Now He Stops • (I Can Recall) Spain • Tones for Joan's Bones • Windows.
00843068 ....$15.95

CHARLES MINGUS Vol. 68
Better Get Hit in Your Soul • Boogie Stop Shuffle • Goodbye Pork Pie Hat • Gunslinging Bird • Jelly Roll • Nostalgia in Times Square • Peggy's Blue Skylight • Pithecanthropus Erectus • Portrait • Slippers.
00843069 ....$16.95

CLASSIC JAZZ Vol. 69
Allen's Alley • Detour Ahead • I Wished on the Moon • Let's Get Lost • Nobody Else but Me • Our Delight • Rockin' in Rhythm • A Sleepin' Bee • Soul Eyes • What Is There to Say.
00843071 ....$14.95

THE DOORS Vol. 70
Break on Through to the Other Side • The End • Hello, I Love You (Won't You Tell Me Your Name?) • L.A. Woman • Light My Fire • Love Me Two Times • People Are Strange • Riders on the Storm • Roadhouse Blues • Touch Me.
00843072 ....$14.95

COLE PORTER CLASSICS Vol. 71
Dream Dancing • From This Moment On • I Get a Kick out of You • I Love Paris • I've Got My Eyes on You • Just One of Those Things • Love for Sale • My Heart Belongs to Daddy • Night and Day • What Is This Thing Called Love?
00843073 ....$14.95

CLASSIC JAZZ BALLADS Vol. 72
For Heaven's Sake • Isfahan • Lament • Maybe You'll Be There • The Single Petal of a Rose • Some Other Spring • Sure Thing • Too Young to Go Steady • You're Looking at Me • You've Changed.
00843074 ....$14.95

JAZZ/BLUES Vol. 73
Break Out the Blues • Bremond's Blues • Gee Baby, Ain't I Good to You • I'll Close My Eyes • Movin' Along (Sid's Twelve) • Night Lights • Reunion Blues • The Sermon • Sunny • This Here.
00843075 ....$14.95

The Hal Leonard JAZZ PLAY-ALONG SERIES is the ultimate learning tool for all jazz musicians. With musician-friendly lead sheets, melody cues and other split track choices on the included CD, this first-of-its-kind package makes learning to play jazz easier and more fun than ever before.

Prices, contents, and availability subject to change without notice.

FOR MORE INFORMATION,
SEE YOUR LOCAL MUSIC DEALER,
OR WRITE TO:

HAL•LEONARD®
CORPORATION
7777 W. BLUEMOUND RD. P.O. BOX 13819
MILWAUKEE, WISCONSIN 53213

Visit Hal Leonard online at
www.halleonard.com

Jazz Instruction & Improvisation

Books for All Instruments from Hal Leonard

AN APPROACH TO JAZZ IMPROVISATION

by Dave Pozzi
Musicians Institute Press

Explore the styles of Charlie Parker, Sonny Rollins, Bud Powell and others with this comprehensive guide to jazz improvisation. Covers: scale choices • chord analysis • phrasing • melodies • harmonic progressions • more.
00695135 Book/CD Pack $17.95

INCLUDES TAB

BUILDING A JAZZ VOCABULARY

By Mike Steinel

A valuable resource for learning the basics of jazz from Mike Steinel of the University of North Texas. It covers: the basics of jazz • how to build effective solos • a comprehensive practice routine • and a jazz vocabulary of the masters.
00849911 ....$19.95

THE CYCLE OF FIFTHS

by Emile and Laura De Cosmo

This essential instruction book provides more than 450 exercises, including hundreds of melodic and rhythmic ideas. The book is designed to help improvisors master the cycle of fifths, one of the primary progressions in music. Guaranteed to refine technique, enhance improvisational fluency, and improve sight-reading!
00311114 ....$14.95

THE DIATONIC CYCLE

by Emile and Laura De Cosmo

Renowned jazz educators Emile and Laura De Cosmo provide more than 300 exercises to help improvisors tackle one of music's most common progressions: the diatonic cycle. This book is guaranteed to refine technique, enhance improvisational fluency, and improve sight-reading!
00311115 ....$16.95

EAR TRAINING

by Keith Wyatt,
Carl Schroeder and Joe Elliott
Musicians Institute Press

Covers: basic pitch matching • singing major and minor scales • identifying intervals • transcribing melodies and rhythm • identifying chords and progressions • seventh chords and the blues • modal interchange, chromaticism, modulation • and more.
00695198 Book/2-CD Pack $24.95

EXERCISES AND ETUDES FOR THE JAZZ INSTRUMENTALIST

by J.J. Johnson

Designed as study material and playable by any instrument, these pieces run the gamut of the jazz experience, featuring common and uncommon time signatures and keys, and styles from ballads to funk. They are progressively graded so that both beginners and professionals will be challenged by the demands of this wonderful music.
00842018 Bass Clef Edition $16.95
00842042 Treble Clef Edition $16.95

JAZZOLOGY

THE ENCYCLOPEDIA OF JAZZ THEORY FOR ALL MUSICIANS
by Robert Rawlins and Nor Eddine Bahha

This comprehensive resource covers a variety of jazz topics, for beginners and pros of any instrument. The book serves as an encyclopedia for reference, a thorough methodology for the student, and a workbook for the classroom.
00311167 ....$18.95

JAZZ THEORY RESOURCES

by Bert Ligon
Houston Publishing, Inc.

This is a jazz theory text in two volumes. **Volume 1 includes:** review of basic theory • rhythm in jazz performance • triadic generalization • diatonic harmonic progressions and analysis • substitutions and turnarounds • and more. **Volume 2 includes:** modes and modal frameworks • quartal harmony • extended tertian structures and triadic superimposition • pentatonic applications • coloring "outside" the lines and beyond • and more.
00030458 Volume 1 ....$39.95
00030459 Volume 2 ....$29.95

JOY OF IMPROV

by Dave Frank and John Amaral

This book/CD course on improvisation for all instruments and all styles will help players develop monster musical skills! **Book One** imparts a solid basis in technique, rhythm, chord theory, ear training and improv concepts. **Book Two** explores more advanced chord voicings, chord arranging techniques and more challenging blues and melodic lines. The CD can be used as a listening and play-along tool.
00220005 Book 1 – Book/CD Pack $24.95
00220006 Book 2 – Book/CD Pack $24.95

THE PATH TO JAZZ IMPROVISATION

by Emile and Laura De Cosmo

This fascinating jazz instruction book offers an innovative, scholarly approach to the art of improvisation. It includes in-depth analysis and lessons about: cycle of fifths • diatonic cycle • overtone series • pentatonic scale • harmonic and melodic minor scale • polytonal order of keys • blues and bebop scales • modes • and more.
00310904 ....$14.95

THE SOURCE

THE DICTIONARY OF CONTEMPORARY AND TRADITIONAL SCALES
by Steve Barta

This book serves as an informative guide for people who are looking for good, solid information regarding scales, chords, and how they work together. It provides right and left hand fingerings for scales, chords, and complete inversions. Includes over 20 different scales, each written in all 12 keys.
00240885 ....$15.95

21 BEBOP EXERCISES

by Steve Rawlins

This book/CD pack is both a warm-up collection and a manual for bebop phrasing. Its tasty and sophisticated exercises will help you develop your proficiency with jazz interpretation. It concentrates on practice in all twelve keys – moving higher by half-step – to help develop dexterity and range. The companion CD includes all of the exercises in 12 keys.
00315341 Book/CD Pack $17.95

THE WOODSHEDDING SOURCE BOOK

by Emile De Cosmo

Rehearsing with this method daily will improve technique, reading ability, rhythmic and harmonic vocabulary, eye/finger coordination, endurance, range, theoretical knowledge, and listening skills – all of which lead to superior improvisational skills.
00842000 C Instruments $19.95

FOR MORE INFORMATION, SEE YOUR LOCAL MUSIC DEALER, OR WRITE TO:

HAL•LEONARD®
CORPORATION
7777 W. BLUEMOUND RD. P.O. BOX 13819 MILWAUKEE, WI 53213

Visit Hal Leonard online at
www.halleonard.com

0908

Prices, contents & availability subject to change without notice.

ARTIST TRANSCRIPTIONS

Artist Transcriptions are authentic, note-for-note transcriptions of today's hottest artists in jazz, pop and rock. These outstanding, accurate arrangements are in an easy-to-read format which includes all essential lines. Artist Transcriptions can be used to perform, sequence or for reference.

CLARINET

00672423	Buddy De Franco Collection	$19.95

FLUTE

00672379	Eric Dolphy Collection	$19.95
00672372	James Moody Collection – Sax and Flute	$19.95
00660108	James Newton – Improvising Flute	$14.95
00672455	Lew Tabackin Collection	$19.95

GUITAR & BASS

00660113	The Guitar Style of George Benson	$14.95
00699072	Guitar Book of Pierre Bensusan	$29.95
00672331	Ron Carter – Acoustic Bass	$16.95
00672307	Stanley Clarke Collection	$19.95
00660115	Al Di Meola – Friday Night in San Francisco	$14.95
00604043	Al Di Meola – Music, Words, Pictures	$14.95
00673245	Jazz Style of Tal Farlow	$19.95
00672359	Bela Fleck and the Flecktones	$18.95
00699389	Jim Hall – Jazz Guitar Environments	$19.95
00699306	Jim Hall – Exploring Jazz Guitar	$19.95
00604049	Allan Holdsworth – Reaching for the Uncommon Chord	$14.95
00699215	Leo Kottke – Eight Songs	$14.95
00672356	Jazz Guitar Standards	$19.95
00675536	Wes Montgomery – Guitar Transcriptions	$17.95
00672353	Joe Pass Collection	$18.95
00673216	John Patitucci	$16.95
00027083	Django Reinhardt Anthology	$14.95
00026711	Genius of Django Reinhardt	$10.95
00026715	Django Reinhardt - A Treasury of Songs	$12.95
00672374	Johnny Smith Guitar Solos	$16.95
00672320	Mark Whitfield	$19.95

PIANO & KEYBOARD

00672338	Monty Alexander Collection	$19.95
00672487	Monty Alexander Plays Standards	$19.95
00672318	Kenny Barron Collection	$22.95
00672520	Count Basie Collection	$19.95
00672364	Warren Bernhardt Collection	$19.95
00672439	Cyrus Chestnut Collection	$19.95
00673242	Billy Childs Collection	$19.95
00672300	Chick Corea – Paint the World	$12.95
00672537	Bill Evans at Town Hall	$16.95
00672425	Bill Evans – Piano Interpretations	$19.95
00672365	Bill Evans – Piano Standards	$19.95
00672510	Bill Evans Trio – Vol. 1: 1959-1961	$24.95
00672511	Bill Evans Trio – Vol. 2: 1962-1965	$24.95
00672512	Bill Evans Trio – Vol. 3: 1968-1974	$24.95
00672513	Bill Evans Trio – Vol. 4: 1979-1980	$24.95
00672381	Tommy Flanagan Collection	$19.95
00672492	Benny Goodman Collection	$16.95
00672329	Benny Green Collection	$19.95

00672486	Vince Guaraldi Collection	$19.95
00672419	Herbie Hancock Collection	$19.95
00672438	Hampton Hawes	$19.95
00672322	Ahmad Jamal Collection	$22.95
00672476	Brad Mehldau Collection	$19.95
00672388	Best of Thelonious Monk	$19.95
00672389	Thelonious Monk Collection	$19.95
00672390	Thelonious Monk Plays Jazz Standards – Volume 1	$19.95
00672391	Thelonious Monk Plays Jazz Standards – Volume 2	$19.95
00672433	Jelly Roll Morton – The Piano Rolls	$12.95
00672553	Charlie Parker for Piano	$19.95
00672542	Oscar Peterson – Jazz Piano Solos	$16.95
00672544	Oscar Peterson – Originals	$9.95
00672532	Oscar Peterson – Plays Broadway	$19.95
00672531	Oscar Peterson – Plays Duke Ellington	$19.95
00672533	Oscar Peterson – Trios	$24.95
00672543	Oscar Peterson Trio – Canadiana Suite	$9.95
00672534	Very Best of Oscar Peterson	$22.95
00672371	Bud Powell Classics	$19.95
00672376	Bud Powell Collection	$19.95
00672437	André Previn Collection	$19.95
00672507	Gonzalo Rubalcaba Collection	$19.95
00672303	Horace Silver Collection	$19.95
00672316	Art Tatum Collection	$22.95
00672355	Art Tatum Solo Book	$19.95
00672357	Billy Taylor Collection	$24.95
00673215	McCoy Tyner	$16.95
00672321	Cedar Walton Collection	$19.95
00672519	Kenny Werner Collection	$19.95
00672434	Teddy Wilson Collection	$19.95

SAXOPHONE

00673244	Julian "Cannonball" Adderley Collection	$19.95
00673237	Michael Brecker	$19.95
00672429	Michael Brecker Collection	$19.95
00672447	Best of the Brecker Brothers	$19.95
00672315	Benny Carter Plays Standards	$22.95
00672314	Benny Carter Collection	$22.95
00672394	James Carter Collection	$19.95
00672349	John Coltrane Plays Giant Steps	$19.95
00672529	John Coltrane – Giant Steps	$14.95
00672494	John Coltrane – A Love Supreme	$14.95
00672493	John Coltrane Plays "Coltrane Changes"	$19.95
00672453	John Coltrane Plays Standards	$19.95
00673233	John Coltrane Solos	$22.95
00672328	Paul Desmond Collection	$19.95
00672379	Eric Dolphy Collection	$19.95
00672530	Kenny Garrett Collection	$19.95
00699375	Stan Getz	$19.95
00672377	Stan Getz – Bossa Novas	$19.95
00672375	Stan Getz – Standards	$18.95
00673254	Great Tenor Sax Solos	$18.95
00672523	Coleman Hawkins Collection	$19.95

00673252	Joe Henderson – Selections from "Lush Life" & "So Near So Far"	$19.95
00672330	Best of Joe Henderson	$22.95
00673239	Best of Kenny G	$19.95
00673229	Kenny G – Breathless	$19.95
00672462	Kenny G – Classics in the Key of G	$19.95
00672485	Kenny G – Faith: A Holiday Album	$14.95
00672373	Kenny G – The Moment	$19.95
00672326	Joe Lovano Collection	$19.95
00672498	Jackie McLean Collection	$19.95
00672372	James Moody Collection – Sax and Flute	$19.95
00672416	Frank Morgan Collection	$19.95
00672539	Gerry Mulligan Collection	$19.95
00672352	Charlie Parker Collection	$19.95
00672561	Best of Sonny Rollins	$19.95
00672444	Sonny Rollins Collection	$19.95
00675000	David Sanborn Collection	$17.95
00672528	Bud Shank Collection	$19.95
00672491	New Best of Wayne Shorter	$19.95
00672455	Lew Tabackin Collection	$19.95
00672350	Tenor Saxophone Standards	$18.95
00672334	Stanley Turrentine Collection	$19.95
00672524	Lester Young Collection	$19.95

TROMBONE

00672332	J.J. Johnson Collection	$19.95
00672489	Steve Turré Collection	$19.95

TRUMPET

00672557	Herb Alpert Collection	$14.95
00672480	Louis Armstrong Collection	$17.95
00672481	Louis Armstrong Plays Standards	$17.95
00672435	Chet Baker Collection	$19.95
00672556	Best of Chris Botti	$19.95
00673234	Randy Brecker	$17.95
00672447	Best of the Brecker Brothers	$19.95
00672448	Miles Davis – Originals, Vol. 1	$19.95
00672451	Miles Davis – Originals, Vol. 2	$19.95
00672450	Miles Davis – Standards, Vol. 1	$19.95
00672449	Miles Davis – Standards, Vol. 2	$19.95
00672479	Dizzy Gillespie Collection	$19.95
00673214	Freddie Hubbard	$14.95
00672382	Tom Harrell – Jazz Trumpet	$19.95
00672363	Jazz Trumpet Solos	$9.95
00672506	Chuck Mangione Collection	$19.95
00672525	Arturo Sandoval – Trumpet Evolution	$19.95

FOR MORE INFORMATION, SEE YOUR LOCAL MUSIC DEALER, OR WRITE TO:

HAL•LEONARD®
CORPORATION
7777 W. BLUEMOUND RD. P.O. BOX 13819 MILWAUKEE, WI 53213

Visit our web site for a complete listing of our titles with songlists at
www.halleonard.com

Prices and availability subject to change without notice.

NOTE-FOR-NOTE TRANSCRIPTIONS • FROM THE ORIGINAL RECORDINGS •

transcribed horns

Imagine playing the exact parts of some of the most memorable and consequential songs of our time note-for-note, exactly as the legends played them. This unique new series features transcriptions of all the horn parts included on the original recordings.

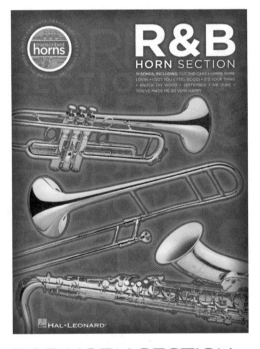

FUNK/DISCO HORN SECTION

15 classics: Brick House • Disco Inferno • Dr. Funkenstein • Fire • Give It to Me Baby • Hold On I'm Comin' • Lucretia Mac Evil • Papa's Got a Brand New Bag • Pick up the Pieces • Serpentine Fire • Superstition • That's the Way (I Like It) • Y.M.C.A. • You Should Be Dancing • What Is Hip.
_____00001148 ....$19.95

POP/ROCK HORN SECTION

15 great hits: Bright Side of the Road • Higher Love • Hot Hot Hot • The Impression That I Get • Jump, Jive An' Wail • Livin' La Vida Loca • Magical Mystery Tour • Peg • Smooth • Spinning Wheel • Sussudio • 25 or 6 to 4 • Vehicle • Will It Go Round in Circles • Zoot Suit Riot.
_____00001149 ....$19.95

R&B HORN SECTION

15 R&B standards: Cut the Cake • Dancing in the Street • Gimme Some Lovin' • Hallelujah I Love Him So • Hard to Handle • I Got You (I Feel Good) • In the Midnight Hour • It's Your Thing • Knock on Wood • Mustang Sally • September • Sir Duke • Soul Finger • Soul Man • You've Made Me So Very Happy.
_____00001147 ....$19.95

FOR MORE INFORMATION, SEE YOUR LOCAL MUSIC DEALER, OR WRITE TO:

HAL•LEONARD® CORPORATION

7777 W. BLUEMOUND RD. P.O. BOX 13819 MILWAUKEE, WI 53213
www.halleonard.com

Prices, contents and availability subject to change without notice.